Knowledge of SELF (Social Empowerment Learning Framework)

High School Edition — Facilitator's Guide

™

Developed by: Cedric A. Washington

Author | Educator | Educational Consultant

TEDx Speaker | Founder of NERD Youth Services, Inc.

Knowledge of SELF Curriculum — High School Facilitator's Guide

Who Lives Like This?! Publishing LLC
www.nerdyouthservices.org

ISBN: 978-1-970680-13-3 (Paperback)

Cover design and interior layout by
Who Lives Like This?! Publishing LLC Design Team

Printed in the United States of America

First Edition — 2025

Table of Contents

TM

Unit 5

Good People Skills

TM

About the Author

Cedric A. Washington is a master educator, speaker, author, former college basketball player, and the Executive Director of NERD Youth Services, Inc. A native of Gary, Indiana. Over two decades of experience in education, mentoring, and community leadership have fueled his commitment to building culturally responsive, empowering programs for African American youth. As the visionary behind the Knowledge of SELF (Social Empowerment Learning Framework) curriculum, Cedric blends historical awareness, emotional intelligence, leadership training, and personal reflection to cultivate greatness in every student he reaches. His work has been celebrated nationally at education conferences, faith institutions, and youth leadership summits. Cedric's mission is simple but powerful: To equip young people with the self-knowledge, discipline, and purpose they need to transform themselves — and the world.

Knowledge of SELF Curriculum

Bonus Tools & Supporting Resources

Middle School, High School, and Young Adult Editions

By Cedric A. Washington

"Speak it. Believe it. Do it."

Daily Affirmations

I AM a trailblazer. I AM destined to succeed. Speak it. Believe it. Do it. – Cedric A. Washington

- I am enough, just as I am.
- My history is powerful, my future is greater.
- I am not what the world calls me—I am who God created me to be.
- I will lead with love, courage, and clarity.
- My skin, my hair, my mind—divinely designed.
- I rise above every label and lie.
- Greatness is not ahead of me; it's within me.
- I walk in wisdom and purpose.
- I am part of a legacy of excellence.
- I build, I uplift, I transform.

Icebreaker Activity Bank

Identity Shields

Students draw a shield divided into 4 parts: family, culture, goals, and values.

Affirmation Circle

Each student shares one positive word about themselves. Then peers affirm each person.

If You Really Knew Me

In a safe circle, students complete the sentence: 'If you really knew me, you'd know...'

Who's in Your Circle?

Draw a circle of influence. Identify family, friends, mentors who shape your SELF.

Two Truths and a Dream

Students share two true things about themselves and one aspirational goal.

Pre-Reflection Survey

Before starting the Knowledge of SELF curriculum, please answer honestly:

1. What do you currently know about your cultural identity?

2. How confident are you in making positive decisions for your future? (1–5)

3. What does success mean to you?

4. Have you ever felt misunderstood in school or in life? Explain.

5. What do you hope to gain from this experience?

Post-Reflection Survey

After completing the Knowledge of SELF curriculum, reflect on the following:

1. What is something new you learned about yourself?

2. How has your definition of success changed?

3. What parts of your identity do you embrace more now than before?

4. What are three personal goals you now feel ready to achieve?

5. How will you use what you've learned to uplift others?

Certificate of Completion

This certifies that

_____

has successfully completed the

Knowledge of SELF Curriculum

Middle School / High School / Young Adult Edition

Led by: _____

Date: _____

Created by Cedric A. Washington | "Speak it. Believe it. Do it."

TM

Knowledge of SELF (Social Empowerment Learning Framework)

High School Edition — Facilitator's Guide ™

Unit One: SELF Conscience

Lesson 1: Am I a Color? (Part 1)

Objective:
Students will critically examine identity labels and explore the concept of ethnic versus national identity.

Do Now:
Do you recognize yourself as African American? If yes, what does that mean to you?

_____

_____

_____

_____

_____

_____

_____

_____

_____

_____

Facilitator's Talk:
Introduce historical labels: Nigger, Negro, Colored, Black, African American. Discuss how these terms shaped identity confusion.
Lead into definitions:
- Ethnicity: Cultural identity.
- Nationality: Legal allegiance to a nation.

Mini-Lesson Key Points:
- Africa is a continent with 54 countries.
- African American is often used without true geographical or cultural connection.
- Bible references as historical text (Genesis 6–10, Genesis 42:6–8, Exodus 2:19, Deuteronomy 28, Revelation 1:14-15).

Key Discussion Questions:
1. Does being called African American tell you your true origin?
2. How does knowing or not knowing your true history impact your self-esteem?

Activity:
Students reflect in writing: "Who am I beyond a label?"

Real World Connection:
Discuss the separation of historical truth from education (separation of church and state).

Reflection Journal:

What part of today's conversation made you rethink your own identity?
[Write two full paragraphs.]

_____
_____
_____
_____
_____
_____
_____
_____
_____
_____
_____
_____
_____
_____
_____
_____
_____
_____
_____
_____
_____
_____
_____
_____
_____
_____
_____
_____
_____
_____
_____
_____
_____

Lesson 2: Am I a Color? (Part 2)

Objective:
Students will continue building identity awareness and critically examine terms like Black and White.

Do Now:
What is the purpose of going to church? What is the purpose of going to school? List two things both have in common.

_____
_____
_____
_____
_____
_____
_____
_____
_____
_____
_____

Facilitator's Talk:
Discuss the Bible as a historical document. Reconnect to Deuteronomy 28 and the prophecy regarding 400 years of oppression.
Discuss the Trans-Atlantic Slave Trade using historical sources.

Mini-Lesson Key Points:
- Slavery was not the beginning of African people's history.
- Bible historical connections lost through separation of state and religion.

Key Discussion Questions:
1. Why is it powerful to reconnect African Americans to ancient history?
2. How has miseducation about identity impacted our communities?

Activity:
Have students read a selected passage from Deuteronomy 28. Write a response connecting it to their knowledge of American history.

Real World Connection:
Watch excerpt from the documentary on Trans-Atlantic Slave Trade and discuss.

Reflection Journal:

How would education change if true African history was taught from the beginning?
[Write two full paragraphs.]

_____
_____
_____
_____
_____
_____
_____
_____
_____
_____
_____
_____
_____
_____
_____
_____
_____
_____
_____
_____
_____
_____
_____
_____
_____
_____
_____
_____
_____
_____
_____
_____
_____

Lesson 3: Love Yourself — The Skin You're In

Objective:
Students will embrace self-love by understanding melanin and rejecting negative self-perceptions.

Do Now:
Have you ever heard or said, "I don't want to get too dark"? Why do you think that is?

_____

Facilitator's Talk:
Teach the power of melanin: pigment that protects and strengthens. Explain melanin's structure (6 protons, 6 electrons, 6 neutrons — "666" misrepresented in media).
Use the Skin Tone Chart: Students find their hue of brown — reinforcing that no one is truly "black" or "white."

Color Me Human | Skin Tone Chart   expl◯ratorium™

A1	B1	C1	D1	E1	F1
A2	B2	C2	D2	E2	F2
A3	B3	C3	D3	E3	F3
A4	B4	C4	D4	E4	E4
A5	B5	C5	D5	E5	E5
A6	B6	C6	D6	E6	E6
A7	B7	C7	D7	E7	E7
A8	B8	C8	D8	E8	E8
A9	B9	C9	D9	E9	E9
A10	B10	C10	D10	E10	E10
A11	B11	C11	D11	E11	E11

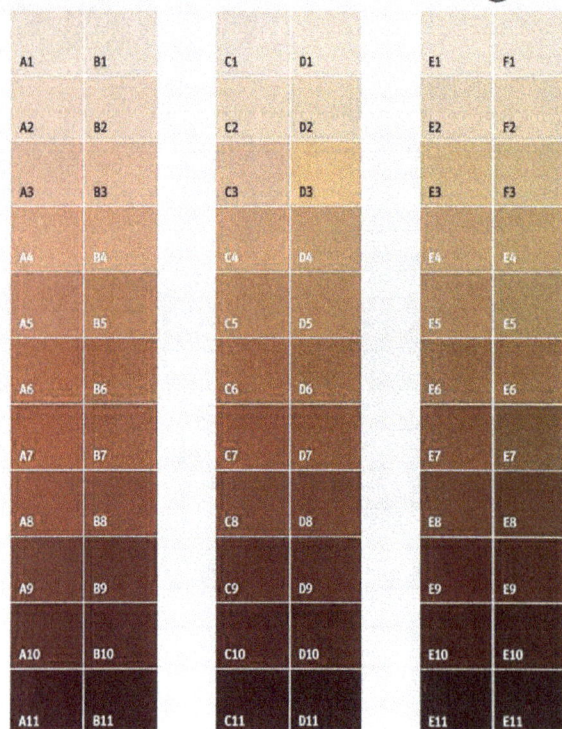

Mini-Lesson Key Points:
- Melanin is divine power.
- Words have power: Examine definitions of "black" and "white" from the dictionary.

Key Discussion Questions:
1. How does redefining your complexion change the way you see yourself?
2. Why must we control the words and labels we accept about ourselves?

Activity:
Define "black" and "white" using Merriam-Webster dictionary. Write how these definitions differ from how you want to be described.

Real World Connection:
Research how ancient African civilizations celebrated skin, culture, and royalty.

Reflection Journal:
What is something you now love more about yourself after today's lesson?
[Write two full paragraphs.]

_____
_____

_____
_____
_____
_____
_____
_____
_____
_____
_____
_____
_____
_____
_____
_____
_____
_____
_____
_____
_____
_____
_____
_____
_____
_____
_____
_____
_____
_____

Lesson 4: Attributes/Characteristics of SELF

Objective:
Students will explore personal attributes and build self-awareness through critical reflection.

Do Now:
What are three positive qualities you see in yourself?

_____
_____
_____
_____
_____
_____
_____
_____
_____
_____
_____
_____

Facilitator's Talk:
Discuss the importance of understanding personal strengths, quirks, and areas of growth.

Mini-Lesson Key Points:
- Attributes shape your behavior and decisions.
- Self-awareness leads to empowerment.

Key Discussion Questions:
1. Why is it important to know your own attributes and characteristics?
2. How do personal traits influence your leadership and success?

Activity:
Self-Inventory: Students list 5 strengths and 2 areas they want to improve.

Real World Connection:
Study leaders or icons students admire and identify their key personal characteristics.

Reflection Journal:
Which personal attribute do you believe will help you leave a legacy?
[Write two full paragraphs.]

_____
_____
_____
_____
_____
_____
_____
_____
_____
_____
_____
_____
_____
_____
_____
_____
_____
_____
_____
_____
_____
_____
_____
_____
_____
_____
_____
_____
_____
_____
_____
_____
_____
_____

Lesson 5: Ethics

Objective:
Students will define their core values and understand how ethics guide choices and leadership.

Do Now:
List three values that are very important to you.

_____

_____

_____

_____

_____

_____

_____

_____

_____

_____

_____

_____

_____

Facilitator's Talk:
Discuss how ethics reflect what we stand for — even when nobody is watching.

Mini-Lesson Key Points:
- Ethics is choosing integrity over comfort.
- Your actions reflect your principles.

Key Discussion Questions:
1. Why is living by your ethics essential for real leadership?
2. How can sticking to your ethics impact your relationships and future?

Activity:
Personal Ethics Statement: Write a brief paragraph describing your ethical code.

Real World Connection:
Study examples of famous leaders who upheld or betrayed their ethics and the consequences.

Reflection Journal:
What ethical principle will you never compromise on?
[Write two full paragraphs.]

_____
_____
_____
_____
_____
_____
_____
_____
_____
_____
_____
_____
_____
_____
_____
_____
_____
_____
_____
_____
_____
_____
_____
_____
_____
_____
_____
_____
_____
_____
_____
_____
_____

Lesson 6: Image

Objective:
Students will reflect on the difference between public image and private reality and learn to align them authentically.

Do Now:
How do you want people to describe you in one word?

_____
_____
_____
_____
_____
_____
_____
_____
_____
_____
_____
_____
_____
_____

Facilitator's Talk:
Discuss how authentic living — not image management — is the true goal.

Mini-Lesson Key Points:
- Align your public image with your private truth.
- Leadership is about authenticity, not perfection.

Key Discussion Questions:
1. How do social media and society pressure you to project a certain image?
2. Why is being authentic more powerful than being popular?

Activity:
Create Your Authenticity Statement — "I want to be known for..."

Real World Connection:
Analyze examples of public figures who have remained authentic versus those who changed for popularity.

Reflection Journal:
How will you protect your true self as you grow and evolve?
[Write two full paragraphs.]

_____
_____
_____
_____
_____
_____
_____
_____
_____
_____
_____
_____
_____
_____
_____
_____
_____
_____
_____
_____
_____
_____
_____
_____
_____
_____
_____
_____
_____
_____
_____
_____
_____
_____
_____
_____
_____
_____
_____
_____
_____

Lesson 7: Achievements

Objective:
Students will celebrate accomplishments and set higher visions for lifelong achievement.

Do Now:
Name one thing you have accomplished that you are proud of.

_____
_____
_____
_____
_____
_____
_____
_____
_____
_____
_____
_____
_____
_____

Facilitator's Talk:
Teach that achievements aren't just trophies — they are stepping stones to greater purposes.

Mini-Lesson Key Points:
- Acknowledge the small wins as well as the big ones.
- Every achievement builds your self-trust.

Key Discussion Questions:
1. Why is it important to celebrate progress, not just perfection?
2. How can reflecting on past achievements fuel your future goals?

Activity:
Victory Log — List 5 achievements you are proud of and what they taught you.

Real World Connection:
Study successful people and notice how early achievements helped launch their futures.

Reflection Journal:
What achievement are you chasing next, and why?
[Write two full paragraphs.]

_____
_____
_____
_____
_____
_____
_____
_____
_____
_____
_____
_____
_____
_____
_____
_____
_____
_____
_____
_____
_____
_____
_____
_____
_____
_____
_____
_____
_____
_____
_____
_____
_____

Knowledge of SELF (Social Empowerment Learning Framework)

High School Edition — Facilitator's Guide ™

Unit Two: SELF Governing

Lesson 1: Health and Nutrition

Objective:
Students will understand the importance of maintaining health and wellness through mindful nutrition.

Do Now:
What is one healthy food you like and one unhealthy food you eat often?

_____

_____

_____

_____

_____

_____

_____

_____

_____

_____

_____

_____

_____

_____

_____

Facilitator's Talk:
Discuss the significance of sea moss, natural remedies, and how ancient cultures valued food as medicine.

Mini-Lesson Key Points:
- Health is wealth: Without it, dreams cannot be achieved.
- Sea moss, fruits, vegetables, and water are essentials for vitality.

Key Discussion Questions:
1. How does nutrition affect your mind, energy, and emotions?
2. Why is health a form of self-respect and self-governance?

Activity:
Build a Daily Health Plan — Identify simple ways to improve diet, hydration, and movement.

Real World Connection:
Study traditional African and Indigenous foods for their healing properties.

Reflection Journal:
What new habit will you commit to for better health?
[Write two full paragraphs.]

_____
_____
_____
_____
_____
_____
_____
_____
_____
_____
_____
_____
_____
_____
_____
_____
_____
_____
_____
_____
_____
_____
_____
_____
_____
_____
_____
_____
_____
_____
_____
_____
_____
_____

Lesson 2: The Importance of FOCUS

Objective:
Students will learn how to cultivate FOCUS using the Knowledge of SELF framework:
Fallback, Opportunities, Cultivate, Understanding, Succeed.

Do Now:
Describe a time when you struggled to stay focused. What distracted you?

_____
_____
_____
_____
_____
_____
_____
_____
_____
_____
_____
_____
_____
_____
_____
_____

Facilitator's Talk:
Explain Cedric A. Washington's method of FOCUS:
- Fallback: Remove distractions.
- Opportunities: Align yourself with positive environments and mentors.
- Cultivate: Practice and refine your craft.
- Understanding: Accept that everyone won't understand your vision.
- Succeed: Celebrate the milestones along the way.

Mini-Lesson Key Points:
- FOCUS is not natural — it's developed.
- FOCUS leads to vision and vision leads to destiny.

Key Discussion Questions:
1. How can falling back from your comfort zone sharpen your focus?
2. How does understanding the misunderstanding of others empower you?

Activity:
FOCUS Action Plan — Students create personal FOCUS blueprints using the method taught.

Real World Connection:
Watch Cedric A. Washington's TEDx Talk on Focus 'How to use FOCUS to become a Trailblazer' and reflect on key takeaways.

Reflection Journal:
What step of FOCUS will you strengthen most this month?
[Write two full paragraphs.]

_____
_____
_____
_____
_____
_____
_____
_____
_____
_____
_____
_____
_____
_____
_____
_____
_____
_____
_____
_____
_____
_____
_____
_____
_____
_____
_____
_____

Lesson 3: Role Modeling

Objective:
Students will recognize their power to be positive role models in their families, schools, and communities.

Do Now:
Who is a role model you admire? Why?

_____
_____
_____
_____
_____
_____
_____
_____
_____
_____
_____
_____
_____
_____
_____
_____
_____
_____
_____

Facilitator's Talk:
Challenge students to realize — they are already role models whether they know it or not.

Mini-Lesson Key Points:
- Someone is always watching your example.
- Leadership is about actions, not titles.

Key Discussion Questions:
1. What kind of example do you want to set for younger kids watching you?
2. How can you live every day in a way that builds others up?

Activity:
Role Model Challenge — Write a list of 5 traits you want to model for others.

Real World Connection:
Research positive young leaders in the community or nation.

Reflection Journal:
What is one thing you will do differently after realizing the power of being a role model?
[Write two full paragraphs.]

_____
_____
_____
_____
_____
_____
_____
_____
_____
_____
_____
_____
_____
_____
_____
_____
_____
_____
_____
_____
_____
_____
_____
_____
_____
_____
_____
_____
_____
_____

Lesson 4: Hygiene

Objective:
Students will understand how personal hygiene impacts self-respect, health, and leadership perception.

Do Now:
Why do you think hygiene is important for more than just appearance?

_____
_____
_____
_____
_____
_____
_____
_____
_____
_____
_____
_____
_____
_____
_____
_____
_____
_____

Facilitator's Talk:
Discuss hygiene as a form of self-love and professionalism. Cleanliness is preparation for opportunity.

Mini-Lesson Key Points:
- Your appearance reflects your self-respect.
- Good hygiene builds confidence and credibility.

Key Discussion Questions:
1. How does personal hygiene affect how others view you and how you view yourself?
2. How is hygiene connected to leadership?

Activity:
Self-Care Checklist — Students create a checklist for daily personal hygiene and grooming habits.

Real World Connection:
Explore how image and hygiene influence success in professional environments.

Reflection Journal:
How will you level up your personal care as an act of self-respect?
[Write two full paragraphs.]

_____

_____

_____

_____

_____

_____

_____

_____

_____

_____

_____

_____

_____

_____

_____

_____

_____

_____

_____

_____

_____

_____

_____

_____

_____

_____

_____

_____

_____

_____

_____

_____

_____

Lesson 5: Emotional Maturity

Objective:
Students will explore the concept of emotional maturity and its impact on decision-making and relationships.

Do Now:
Describe a time you handled a situation more maturely than you would have a year ago.

_____
_____
_____
_____
_____
_____
_____
_____
_____
_____
_____
_____
_____
_____
_____
_____

Facilitator's Talk:
Teach that emotional maturity is not age — it's wisdom, patience, and resilience.

Mini-Lesson Key Points:
- Emotional reactions can either destroy or build relationships.
- Maturity is mastering your emotions, not suppressing them.

Key Discussion Questions:
1. What are signs that someone is emotionally mature?
2. How can emotional maturity lead to greater opportunities?

Activity:
Emotional Pause Plan — Students create a step-by-step action plan for how to pause and respond wisely in emotional situations.

Real World Connection:
Study examples of leaders who demonstrated emotional maturity during crises.

Reflection Journal:
How will you grow your emotional maturity this year?
[Write two full paragraphs.]

Lesson 6: Puberty

Objective:
Students will understand the physical, emotional, and social changes of puberty and build healthy coping skills.

Do Now:
What is one thing you wish adults talked about more regarding growing up?

_____
_____
_____
_____
_____
_____
_____
_____
_____
_____
_____
_____
_____
_____
_____
_____
_____
_____

Facilitator's Talk:
Break the stigma around puberty. Normalize conversations about body changes, emotional swings, and mental health shifts.

Mini-Lesson Key Points:
- Puberty is natural and universal.
- Learning about your body helps you respect and care for yourself better.

Key Discussion Questions:
1. How does understanding your body help you build confidence?
2. How can we support each other during these changes?

Activity:
My Growth Map — Students journal about the biggest physical, emotional, and mental changes they've noticed and what they've learned.

Real World Connection:
Highlight real-world role models who navigated their coming-of-age with authenticity and grace.

Reflection Journal:
What advice would you give your younger self about growing up?
[Write two full paragraphs.]

_____
_____
_____
_____
_____
_____
_____
_____
_____
_____
_____
_____
_____
_____
_____
_____
_____
_____
_____
_____
_____
_____
_____
_____
_____
_____
_____
_____
_____
_____
_____
_____
_____

Lesson 7: Peer Pressure

Objective:
Students will identify types of peer pressure and develop strategies for making independent, empowered choices.

Do Now:
Have you ever been pressured to do something you didn't feel right about? How did you handle it?

_____

_____

_____

_____

_____

_____

_____

_____

_____

_____

_____

_____

_____

_____

_____

_____

_____

Facilitator's Talk:
Normalize that everyone faces peer pressure — maturity is choosing your own path regardless.

Mini-Lesson Key Points:
- Not all peer pressure is negative — but you must filter wisely.
- True leaders sometimes stand alone.

Key Discussion Questions:
1. Why is it powerful to be the one who says no?
2. How can peer pressure shape your destiny if you aren't careful?

Activity:
Scenario Role Play — Students practice handling different types of pressure situations with wisdom.

Real World Connection:
Study leaders who faced criticism but stayed true to their values.

Reflection Journal:
What boundary will you strengthen to protect yourself from negative pressure?
[Write two full paragraphs.]

_____

_____

_____

_____

_____

_____

_____

_____

_____

_____

_____

_____

_____

_____

_____

_____

_____

_____

_____

_____

_____

_____

_____

_____

_____

_____

_____

_____

_____

_____

Knowledge of SELF (Social Empowerment Learning Framework)

High School Edition — Facilitator's Guide

Unit Three: Social Conscience

Lesson 1: How to Be Effective in Your Community

Objective:
Students will learn the importance of service, leadership, and active participation in their communities.

Do Now:
What is one problem in your community you would love to solve?

_____
_____
_____
_____
_____
_____
_____
_____
_____
_____
_____
_____
_____
_____
_____
_____

Facilitator's Talk:
Discuss the idea that real change starts with engaged individuals willing to serve and sacrifice.

Mini-Lesson Key Points:
- Leadership is service, not status.
- Effective leaders listen before they lead.

Key Discussion Questions:
1. Why is it important to know the needs of your community before trying to fix it?
2. How can small acts of service lead to big changes?

Activity:
Community Action Plan — Students design a simple project to impact their school or neighborhood.

Real World Connection:
Research youth-led initiatives that have changed their communities.

Reflection Journal:
What legacy of service do you want to leave in your community?
[Write two full paragraphs.]

_____
_____
_____
_____
_____
_____
_____
_____
_____
_____
_____
_____
_____
_____
_____
_____
_____
_____
_____
_____
_____
_____
_____
_____
_____
_____
_____
_____
_____
_____

Lesson 2: African American Leaders

Objective:
Students will examine the leadership styles, sacrifices, and legacies of influential African American leaders.

Do Now:
Name a Black leader who inspires you. Why?

_____

Facilitator's Talk:
Honor the trailblazers who sacrificed comfort for freedom, education, civil rights, and cultural pride.

Mini-Lesson Key Points:
- Leadership comes in many forms: activism, entrepreneurship, education, the arts.
- Every generation must raise up new leaders.

Key Discussion Questions:
1. What are common traits among great African American leaders?
2. How can studying their lives fuel your leadership journey?

Activity:
Leader Legacy Profiles — Students research and present on an African American leader of their choice.

Real World Connection:
Discuss modern African American leaders making an impact today.

Reflection Journal:
What leadership traits will you cultivate in yourself based on what you learned?
[Write two full paragraphs.]

_____

_____

Lesson 3: Hip Hop: The Culture

Objective:
Students will explore Hip Hop as a cultural movement that blends art, activism, and identity.

Do Now:
How has Hip Hop influenced your life, community, or way of thinking?

_____
_____
_____
_____
_____
_____
_____
_____
_____
_____
_____
_____
_____
_____
_____
_____
_____

Facilitator's Talk:
Break down the four elements of Hip Hop: DJing, MCing, Breaking, Graffiti. Discuss Hip Hop's roots in storytelling, empowerment, and resistance.

Mini-Lesson Key Points:
- Hip Hop was born from struggle, creativity, and hope.
- Real Hip Hop uplifts, educates, and tells truth.

Key Discussion Questions:
1. How has Hip Hop been a voice for marginalized communities?
2. How can we protect the positive roots of Hip Hop culture today?

Activity:
Cultural Impact Map — Students create a visual showing Hip Hop's influence on culture, fashion, activism, and language.

Real World Connection:
Analyze how artists like KRS-One, Tupac, Queen Latifah, J. Cole, and Kendrick Lamar use Hip Hop as social commentary.

Reflection Journal:
How will you use your voice to inspire change like the original Hip Hop pioneers?
[Write two full paragraphs.]

_____

_____

_____

_____

_____

_____

_____

_____

_____

_____

_____

_____

_____

_____

_____

_____

_____

_____

_____

_____

_____

_____

_____

_____

_____

_____

_____

_____

_____

_____

_____

_____

Lesson 4: Family Dynamics

Objective:
Students will explore the impact of family structure, tradition, and values on personal development.

Do Now:
How has your family shaped the way you see the world?

_____
_____
_____
_____
_____
_____
_____
_____
_____
_____
_____
_____
_____
_____
_____
_____
_____
_____
_____

Facilitator's Talk:
Honor the truth that family can be a source of strength or struggle — and still shape greatness.

Mini-Lesson Key Points:
- Family dynamics are foundational to identity.
- Healing and leadership often start within families.

Key Discussion Questions:
1. How have your family's lessons or experiences molded who you are?
2. How can you break negative cycles while honoring positive traditions?

Activity:
Family Reflection Tree — Students create a family values tree: Roots (traditions), Trunk (values), Branches (future goals).

Real World Connection:
Study historical movements that centered around families and communities uniting for strength.

Reflection Journal:
What cycle or tradition in your family will you continue, and why?
[Write two full paragraphs.]

_____
_____
_____
_____
_____
_____
_____
_____
_____
_____
_____
_____
_____
_____
_____
_____
_____
_____
_____
_____
_____
_____
_____
_____
_____
_____
_____
_____
_____
_____
_____
_____

Lesson 5: Accountability

Objective:
Students will understand accountability as a pillar of leadership, maturity, and freedom.

Do Now:
Describe a time when taking responsibility changed the outcome of a situation.

_____
_____
_____
_____
_____
_____
_____
_____
_____
_____
_____
_____
_____
_____
_____
_____
_____
_____

Facilitator's Talk:
Accountability is power — owning your actions means controlling your destiny.

Mini-Lesson Key Points:
- Accountability strengthens trust and self-respect.
- Leaders don't make excuses; they make adjustments.

Key Discussion Questions:
1. How does accountability set you apart from the average person?
2. Why is admitting mistakes a sign of strength, not weakness?

Activity:
Accountability Reflection — Students write about a situation where they took or failed to take accountability and the lessons learned.

Real World Connection:
Research leaders who rose after public mistakes through accountability.

Reflection Journal:
How will you commit to a higher level of accountability moving forward?
[Write two full paragraphs.]

Lesson 6: Community Service and Giving Back

Objective:
Students will discover the power of service as a core part of leadership and building social capital.

Do Now:
Have you ever volunteered or helped someone without being asked? How did it feel?

_____
_____
_____
_____
_____
_____
_____
_____
_____
_____
_____
_____
_____
_____
_____
_____
_____
_____

Facilitator's Talk:
Service connects purpose to power — we rise by lifting others.

Mini-Lesson Key Points:
- True leaders serve before they command.
- Giving back strengthens character and legacy.

Key Discussion Questions:
1. Why does serving others also serve your own growth?
2. How does consistent service change the way others see you and trust you?

Activity:
Service Project Brainstorm — Students design a service project idea they could lead in their school or community.

Real World Connection:
Study leaders who started their journey through local service (e.g., Barack Obama, Dr. King).

Reflection Journal:
What cause will you dedicate your time, talents, or heart to serve?
[Write two full paragraphs.]

_____
_____
_____
_____
_____
_____
_____
_____
_____
_____
_____
_____
_____
_____
_____
_____
_____
_____
_____
_____
_____
_____
_____
_____
_____
_____
_____
_____
_____
_____
_____
_____
_____
_____
_____
_____
_____
_____

Lesson 7: Building Your Legacy

Objective:
Students will define their personal legacy and identify ways to intentionally build it starting now.

Do Now:
If someone described your impact 10 years from now, what would you want them to say?

_____
_____
_____
_____
_____
_____
_____
_____
_____
_____
_____
_____
_____
_____
_____
_____
_____
_____

Facilitator's Talk:
Legacy is built daily — in small acts, in quiet sacrifices, in invisible seeds planted over time.

Mini-Lesson Key Points:
- Legacy is not what you leave for people, but what you leave in people.
- Living with legacy in mind brings focus, meaning, and power.

Key Discussion Questions:
1. How does thinking about legacy influence your daily choices?
2. What is one thing you can do now to start building your legacy?

Activity:
Legacy Vision Board — Students create a visual representation of the life impact they want to leave behind.

Real World Connection:
Study how activists, artists, inventors, and leaders shaped history through legacy-minded living.

Reflection Journal:
What story are you writing with your life today?
[Write two full paragraphs.]

_____

_____

_____

_____

_____

_____

_____

_____

_____

_____

_____

_____

_____

_____

_____

_____

_____

_____

_____

_____

_____

_____

_____

_____

_____

_____

_____

_____

_____

_____

_____

Knowledge of SELF (Social Empowerment Learning Framework)

High School Edition — Facilitator's Guide

TM

Unit Four: Aspirations

Lesson 1: What I Want to Be When I Grow Up

Objective:
Students will begin envisioning their future careers and passions with clarity and purpose.

Do Now:
If you could wake up tomorrow doing any career, what would it be and why?

_____
_____
_____
_____
_____
_____
_____
_____
_____
_____
_____
_____
_____
_____
_____
_____
_____
_____
_____

Facilitator's Talk:
Dreaming big is the first step to achieving big. If you can see it, you can seize it.

Mini-Lesson Key Points:
- Your dream job should align with your talents and passion.
- It's never too early to plan.

Key Discussion Questions:
1. How do your natural skills and interests connect to future career possibilities?
2. Why is purpose more important than chasing a paycheck?

Activity:
Career Vision Statement — Students draft a short paragraph about the career they desire and the impact they want to make.

Real World Connection:
Study how figures like Dr. Mae Jemison and Tyler Perry pursued their dreams despite obstacles.

Reflection Journal:
What steps can you start taking now to prepare for your dream career?
[Write two full paragraphs.]

_____
_____
_____
_____
_____
_____
_____
_____
_____
_____
_____
_____
_____
_____
_____
_____
_____
_____
_____
_____
_____
_____
_____
_____
_____
_____
_____
_____
_____
_____
_____

Lesson 2: Career Day Panel Preparation and Event

Objective:
Students will prepare for and engage in a Career Day event to connect with real-world professionals.

Do Now:
What is one question you would love to ask someone successful in your dream career?

_____

_____

_____

_____

_____

_____

_____

_____

_____

_____

_____

_____

_____

_____

_____

_____

_____

Facilitator's Talk:
Exposure expands possibilities. The right conversation can unlock a destiny.

Mini-Lesson Key Points:
- Preparation shows respect and professionalism.
- Networking is building real relationships, not just asking for favors.

Key Discussion Questions:
1. What is one thing you hope to gain from Career Day?
2. How can you leave a positive impression on a professional mentor?

Activity:
Career Day Question Sheet — Students prepare 5 thoughtful questions for panelists.

Role-play introductions and handshakes.

Real World Connection:
Prepare students for Career Day by researching each guest speaker's career path.

Reflection Journal:
After Career Day, what inspired you most about the experience?
[Write two full paragraphs.]

_____
_____
_____
_____
_____
_____
_____
_____
_____
_____
_____
_____
_____
_____
_____
_____
_____
_____
_____
_____
_____
_____
_____
_____
_____
_____

Lesson 3: Resume Workshop

Objective:
Students will create their first professional resumes to prepare for internships, jobs, and scholarships.

Do Now:
Why do you think first impressions (on paper or in person) are so important?

_____
_____
_____
_____
_____
_____
_____
_____
_____
_____
_____
_____
_____
_____
_____
_____
_____
_____
_____
_____

Facilitator's Talk:
A resume is your personal commercial — it must highlight your best with clarity and confidence.

Mini-Lesson Key Points:
- Resumes showcase skills, leadership, and growth — not just jobs.
- Every experience (volunteering, clubs, sports) matters.

Key Discussion Questions:
1. What are the strengths and skills you want to highlight most on a resume?
2. How can even small experiences show big potential?

Activity:
Resume Building Session — Students use a template to build their first professional resume.

Real World Connection:
Review real resume examples and critique them for strength and clarity.

Reflection Journal:
What is one accomplishment you will proudly highlight on your resume?
[Write two full paragraphs.]

_____
_____
_____
_____
_____
_____
_____
_____
_____
_____
_____
_____
_____
_____
_____
_____
_____
_____
_____
_____
_____
_____
_____
_____
_____
_____
_____
_____
_____

Lesson 4: Short Term Goals

Objective:
Students will learn to create focused, achievable short-term goals that build momentum toward their dreams.

Do Now:
What is one goal you could accomplish in the next 30 days?

_____
_____
_____
_____
_____
_____
_____
_____
_____
_____

Facilitator's Talk:
Short-term goals are stepping stones — you need them to cross rivers of doubt and fear.

Mini-Lesson Key Points:
- Short goals create immediate wins and confidence.
- SMART goals (Specific, Measurable, Achievable, Relevant, Time-bound) guide success.

Key Discussion Questions:
1. Why is it important to break big dreams into smaller steps?
2. How does accomplishing short goals build discipline and self-trust?

Activity:
Goal-Setting Workshop — Students write 3 short-term goals using the SMART format.

Real World Connection:
Study success stories where small daily habits led to big achievements.

Reflection Journal:
Which short-term goal are you most excited to crush?
[Write two full paragraphs.]

_____
_____
_____
_____
_____
_____
_____
_____
_____
_____
_____
_____
_____
_____
_____
_____
_____
_____
_____
_____
_____
_____
_____
_____
_____
_____
_____
_____
_____
_____
_____
_____
_____
_____
_____
_____

Lesson 5: Long Term Goals

Objective:
Students will envision and plan for major long-term goals, understanding the importance of persistence and vision.

Do Now:
Where do you see yourself in 5–10 years?

_____
_____
_____
_____
_____
_____
_____
_____
_____
_____
_____

Facilitator's Talk:
Long-term goals require faith, patience, and consistent daily action.

Mini-Lesson Key Points:
- Vision fuels endurance.
- Your dream deserves a strategy, not just hope.

Key Discussion Questions:
1. How do long-term goals keep you motivated during setbacks?
2. Why is writing down your vision powerful?

Activity:
Dream Big Blueprint — Students draft their 5-year and 10-year life goals.

Real World Connection:
Review vision board examples from entrepreneurs, activists, and leaders.

Reflection Journal:
What legacy do you want your long-term goals to create?
[Write two full paragraphs.]

_____
_____
_____
_____
_____
_____
_____
_____
_____
_____
_____
_____
_____
_____
_____
_____
_____
_____
_____
_____
_____
_____
_____
_____
_____
_____
_____
_____
_____
_____
_____
_____
_____
_____
_____
_____
_____
_____

Lesson 6: Financial Literacy

Objective:
Students will build basic financial literacy skills essential for independence and wealth-building.

Do Now:
If you had $1,000 right now, how would you spend or invest it?

_____

_____

_____

_____

_____

_____

_____

_____

_____

_____

_____

Facilitator's Talk:
Money is a tool, not a master. Learn the game early, or be played by it.

Mini-Lesson Key Points:
- Budgeting, saving, investing, and financial discipline are keys to freedom.
- Building wealth starts with knowledge, not luck.

Key Discussion Questions:
1. Why is managing small amounts of money now important for managing wealth later?
2. How can financial discipline change your life trajectory?

Activity:
Budget Challenge — Students build a basic monthly budget based on sample incomes.

Real World Connection:
Study young entrepreneurs and investors who built financial independence early.

Reflection Journal:
What is one financial habit you want to develop starting now?
[Write two full paragraphs.]

_____
_____
_____
_____
_____
_____
_____
_____
_____
_____
_____
_____
_____
_____
_____
_____
_____
_____
_____
_____
_____
_____
_____
_____
_____
_____
_____
_____
_____
_____
_____
_____
_____
_____
_____

Lesson 7: Building Wealth and Generational Legacy

Objective:
Students will explore strategies for building wealth and leaving a generational legacy.

Do Now:
What would financial freedom allow you and your family to do?

_____
_____
_____
_____
_____
_____
_____
_____
_____
_____

Facilitator's Talk:
Wealth is not just about money — it's about options, impact, and breaking chains.

Mini-Lesson Key Points:
- Legacy wealth includes money, education, values, and opportunities.
- First-generation wealth builders change bloodlines.

Key Discussion Questions:
1. How does building wealth help build generational power?
2. Why must we think beyond our lifetime when building success?

Activity:
Generational Wealth Map — Students brainstorm ways they can build, protect, and pass on wealth and wisdom.

Real World Connection:
Discuss Black Wall Street and other examples of Black economic empowerment.

Reflection Journal:
What will your financial legacy story be?
[Write two full paragraphs.]

_____
_____
_____
_____
_____
_____
_____
_____
_____
_____
_____
_____
_____
_____
_____
_____
_____
_____
_____
_____
_____
_____
_____
_____
_____
_____
_____
_____
_____
_____
_____
_____
_____

Knowledge of SELF (Social Empowerment Learning Framework)

High School Edition — Facilitator's Guide ™

Unit Five: Good People Skills

Lesson 1: Conflict Resolution

Objective:
Students will learn how to manage and resolve conflict respectfully and constructively.

Do Now:
Describe a time when you successfully solved a disagreement. What worked?

_____
_____
_____
_____
_____
_____
_____
_____
_____
_____
_____

Facilitator's Talk:
Conflict is natural — maturity is handling it wisely.

Mini-Lesson Key Points:
- Most conflicts arise from miscommunication or misunderstanding.
- Listening, empathy, and patience are the keys to resolution.

Key Discussion Questions:
1. Why is resolving conflict peacefully a leadership skill?
2. How does emotional control impact conflict outcomes?

Activity:
Conflict Scenario Role Play — Students practice de-escalating different conflict scenarios.

Real World Connection:
Study peacemakers like Nelson Mandela who turned conflict into transformation.

Reflection Journal:
What will you do differently in your next disagreement to lead with wisdom?
[Write two full paragraphs.]

_____
_____
_____
_____
_____
_____
_____
_____
_____
_____
_____
_____
_____
_____
_____
_____
_____
_____
_____
_____
_____
_____
_____
_____
_____
_____
_____
_____
_____
_____
_____
_____
_____

Lesson 2: Group Cooperation

Objective:
Students will learn the power of collaboration and teamwork.

Do Now:
Think about a time you worked in a group. What made it successful (or not)?

_____
_____
_____
_____
_____
_____
_____
_____
_____
_____
_____
_____

Facilitator's Talk:
None of us can do it alone. Teamwork makes the dream work — but only with communication and shared respect.

Mini-Lesson Key Points:
- Great teams honor different strengths.
- Communication and trust are essential.

Key Discussion Questions:
1. Why is learning to cooperate crucial for leadership?
2. How can you contribute to a team's success without taking over or checking out?

Activity:
Team Challenge — Students complete a group task, practicing communication, delegation, and encouragement.

Real World Connection:
Research how great teams (sports, activism, business) overcame challenges together.

Reflection Journal:
How will you improve your teamwork skills in the next group opportunity?
[Write two full paragraphs.]

_____
_____
_____
_____
_____
_____
_____
_____
_____
_____
_____
_____
_____
_____
_____
_____
_____
_____
_____
_____
_____
_____
_____
_____
_____
_____
_____
_____
_____
_____
_____
_____
_____
_____
_____

Lesson 3: Friendship

Objective:
Students will explore healthy friendship qualities and boundaries.

Do Now:
What is one quality you value most in a friend?

_____
_____
_____
_____
_____
_____
_____
_____
_____
_____
_____
_____
_____

Facilitator's Talk:
Friendships shape your future. Choose wisely — build intentionally.

Mini-Lesson Key Points:
- True friends encourage growth, not destruction.
- Healthy boundaries keep relationships strong and safe.

Key Discussion Questions:
1. What separates a real friend from a fake one?
2. How do healthy friendships help you reach your dreams?

Activity:
Friendship Reflection — Students write about a friendship that made them better or one they had to outgrow.

Real World Connection:
Discuss loyalty and boundaries within famous friendships (e.g., historic movements, sports teams, artist collectives).

Reflection Journal:
What kind of friend do you commit to being from now on?
[Write two full paragraphs.]

Lesson 4: Identifying Unhealthy Relationships

Objective:
Students will learn how to recognize and respond to toxic and unhealthy relationship patterns.

Do Now:
Have you ever had to walk away from a relationship that wasn't good for you? How did it feel?

_____
_____
_____
_____
_____
_____
_____
_____
_____
_____
_____
_____
_____
_____

Facilitator's Talk:
Protecting your peace is just as important as protecting your dreams.

Mini-Lesson Key Points:
- Unhealthy relationships drain your spirit and purpose.
- Love should never come with fear, disrespect, or manipulation.

Key Discussion Questions:
1. What are signs of an unhealthy friendship or relationship?
2. Why is it important to set boundaries, even with people you care about?

Activity:
Relationship Red Flag Map — Students list warning signs to watch for and healthy alternatives.

Real World Connection:
Study examples of people who overcame toxic environments to pursue greatness.

Reflection Journal:
How will you protect your peace moving forward?
[Write two full paragraphs.]

_____

_____

_____

_____

_____

_____

_____

_____

_____

_____

_____

_____

_____

_____

_____

_____

_____

_____

_____

_____

_____

_____

_____

_____

_____

_____

_____

_____

Lesson 5: Self-Love

Objective:
Students will define and practice self-love as the foundation of all other relationships.

Do Now:
What is one thing you genuinely love about yourself?

_____
_____
_____
_____
_____
_____
_____
_____
_____
_____
_____
_____
_____
_____

Facilitator's Talk:
You can only love others as deeply as you love yourself.

Mini-Lesson Key Points:
- Self-love is not arrogance — it's self-respect, self-worth, and self-care.
- It's hard to build healthy relationships without first building a healthy relationship with yourself.

Key Discussion Questions:
1. How does self-love change the way you allow others to treat you?
2. Why is protecting your peace an act of self-love?

Activity:
Self-Love Blueprint — Students write 5 affirmations and 5 self-care promises to themselves.

Real World Connection:
Explore how famous leaders, artists, and changemakers practiced self-love amidst adversity.

Reflection Journal:
What does self-love look like in your daily life?
[Write two full paragraphs.]

Lesson 6: Communication Skills

Objective:
Students will develop essential communication skills for strong personal and professional relationships.

Do Now:
Think of someone you admire for how they communicate. What makes them great?

_____
_____
_____
_____
_____
_____
_____
_____
_____
_____
_____
_____
_____
_____
_____

Facilitator's Talk:
Great communication opens doors that even talent can't unlock.

Mini-Lesson Key Points:
- Listening is just as powerful as speaking.
- Tone, body language, and clarity matter.

Key Discussion Questions:
1. Why is communication a leadership skill?
2. How can listening make you a better leader and friend?

Activity:
Communication Role Play — Students practice active listening and clear speaking exercises.

Real World Connection:
Study speeches and conversations that changed history (e.g., Dr. King's speeches).

Reflection Journal:
What communication skill will you work on improving?
[Write two full paragraphs.]

_____
_____
_____
_____
_____
_____
_____
_____
_____
_____
_____
_____
_____

_____
_____
_____
_____
_____
_____
_____
_____
_____
_____
_____
_____
_____
_____
_____
_____
_____

Lesson 7: Emotional Intelligence

Objective:
Students will understand emotional intelligence (EQ) and why it is critical for success and leadership.

Do Now:
Describe a time when understanding someone's feelings changed how you responded.

_____
_____
_____
_____
_____
_____
_____
_____
_____

Facilitator's Talk:
Success isn't just about IQ — EQ determines how you lead, love, and grow.

Mini-Lesson Key Points:
- EQ is knowing your emotions, managing them, and navigating others' emotions wisely.
- Emotional maturity creates influence and trust.

Key Discussion Questions:
1. How can emotional intelligence help you avoid drama and build better relationships?
2. Why is empathy powerful for leaders?

Activity:
EQ Reflection — Students journal on three ways they will strengthen their emotional intelligence.

Real World Connection:
Analyze how emotionally intelligent leaders have made lasting change.

Reflection Journal:
How will mastering your emotions change your destiny?
[Write two full paragraphs.]

_____
_____
_____
_____
_____

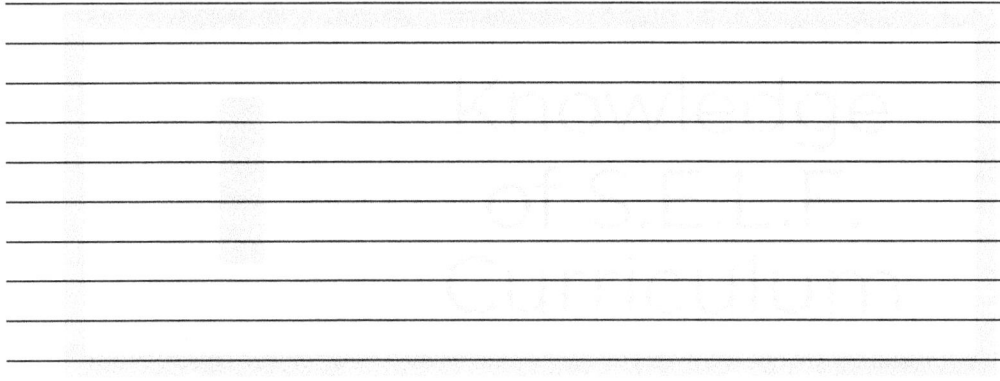

Appendix

SECTION 1 — Curriculum Purpose & Philosophy

The Knowledge of SELF® (Social Empowerment Learning Framework) Curriculum is built on the belief that **identity is the foundation of education**, and that young people thrive when they understand:

- **Who they are**
- **Where they come from**
- **What they carry**
- **Who they were created to be**

Across all editions, the curriculum centers five pillars:

1. **SELF Conscience** – Identity, truth, history, faith, self-love
2. **SELF Governing** – Discipline, focus, purpose, integrity
3. **Social Conscience** – Empathy, justice, unity, allyship
4. **Aspirations** – Vision, goals, legacy, breaking cycles
5. **Good People Skills** – Communication, conflict resolution, emotional intelligence

These pillars are consistent across middle school, high school, and young adult programming.

The curriculum guides youth to:

- Reclaim identity beyond labels and stereotypes
- Understand historical and biblical truths hidden from traditional education
- Build self-worth through cultural pride
- Strengthen discipline and focus
- Lead their lives with purpose
- Develop empathy and advocate for justice
- Dream boldly and build legacy
- Grow strong communication and relationship skills

SECTION 2 — Core Framework: The 5 Units of SELF Mastery

Unit 1: SELF Conscience

Focus:

- Identity
- History before slavery
- Spiritual foundations
- Mental health
- Understanding melanin
- Labels vs. legacy
- Reclaiming truth

Lessons directly include:

- "Am I a Color? Part 1 & 2"
- "Love Yourself — The Skin You're In"
- "Attributes/Characteristic of SELF"
- "Ethics"
- "Image"
- "Achievements"

Unit 2: SELF Governing

Focus:

- Authenticity
- Focus
- Discipline
- Integrity
- Purpose
- Self-assessment

Lessons include:

- "Health and Nutrition"
- "The Importance of Focus"
- "Role Modeling"
- "Hygiene"
- "Emotional Maturity"
- "Puberty"
- "Peer Pressure"

Unit 3: Social Conscience

Focus:

- Justice
- Compassion
- Empathy
- Perspective-taking
- Advocacy
- Unity
- Allyship

Lessons include:

- "How to be Effective in Your Community"
- "African American Leaders"
- "Hip-Hop the Culture"
- "Family Dynamics"
- "Accountability"
- "Community Service and Giving Back"
- "Building Your Legacy"

Unit 4: Aspirations

Focus:

- Dreaming without limits
- Setting goals
- Breaking generational patterns
- Overcoming obstacles
- Role models & mentors
- Becoming a trailblazer

Lessons include:

- "What I Want to be When I Grow Up"
- "Career Day Panel Preparation and Event"
- "Resume Workshop"
- "Short Term Goals"
- "Long Term Goals"
- "Financial Literacy"
- "Building Wealth and Generational Legacy"

Unit 5: Good People Skills

Focus:

- Communication
- Conflict resolution
- Social awareness
- Collaboration
- Manners & respect
- Service & humility

Lessons include:

- ""Conflict Resolution"
- "Group Cooperation"
- "Friendship"
- "Identifying Unhealthy Relationships"
- "SELF Love"
- "Communication Skills"
- "Emotional Intelligence"

SECTION 3 — Instructional Model Embedded in All Lessons

1. Do Now Prompt

Every lesson begins with written reflection in the student's own words.
This establishes relevance, builds student voice, and activates prior knowledge.

2. Vocabulary Focus

Each lesson includes 1–3 high-value academic or cultural terms.
The vocabulary always connects to the identity, empowerment, or behavioral purpose of the

lesson.

3. Mini-Lesson Delivery Tips / Key Points

This section consistently includes:

- Clear explanation of the concept
- Historical or biblical framing
- Identity-based connections
- Real-world relevance

4. Critical Thinking Discussion

Your lessons intentionally challenge students to think deeper about identity, justice, purpose, trauma, and faith.
Guiding questions always center truth, empowerment, and awareness.

5. Activities

Every lesson includes a hands-on, reflective, or creative activity connected directly to identity, leadership, or self-discovery.

Examples include:

- Identity Timeline
- Skin Tone Chart
- Generational Healing Tree
- Purpose Map
- Justice Wall
- Team Tower Challenge

6. Reflection Journals

Reflection is a **signature component** of the KOS curriculum.
Every lesson closes by asking youth to process what they learned about themselves, their purpose, their community, or their future.

7. Unit Check-Ins

Each unit concludes with a structured self-assessment (Growth Wheel, Scorecard, etc.)
These build metacognition, accountability, and transformation.

SECTION 4 — Biblical & Historical Integration

(Using the passages already embedded in your lessons.)

Scriptural references in your curriculum appear **consistently and purposefully**, including:

- **Genesis 6-10**
- **Genesis 42:6-8**
- **Exodus 2:19**
- **Deuteronomy 28**
- **Revelation 1:14-15**

These passages come **directly from your lessons**, grounding the curriculum in:

- Spiritual empowerment
- Identity reclamation
- Historical truth
- Moral guidance
- Leadership development

SECTION 5 — Universal Assessment Tools & Reflection Systems

The Knowledge of SELF® Curriculum uses an assessment system that is consistent across all editions—Middle School, High School, and Young Adult. Your assessments focus on:

- **Identity development**
- **Self-awareness**
- **Growth over time**
- **Purpose-driven decision-making**
- **Emotional intelligence**
- **Historical and spiritual grounding**

5.1 — Do Now Written Reflections

Every lesson in the curriculum begins with a **Do Now reflection prompt**, asking students to write paragraphs that connect personally to the lesson's theme.

Examples taken directly from the lessons include:

- "Do you recognize yourself as an African American? What does that mean to you personally?"
- "What distracts you the most from your goals?"
- "Have you ever judged someone before knowing their story?"
- "What would you do or be if nothing could stop you?"
- "What's one issue in the world or your school that bothers you? Why?"
- "What does respect look like in action?"

These reflective writings function as:

- **Baseline assessments**
- **Identity checks**
- **SEL awareness indicators**
- **Tools for measuring growth across units**

5.2 — Vocabulary Mastery

Every lesson includes key terms that reinforce academic language, cultural understanding, and identity development.

Your vocabulary lists include terms such as:

- Ethnicity
- Nationality
- Melanin
- Trauma
- Integrity
- Empathy
- Vision
- Leadership
- Unity
- Perspective
- Communication
- Courtesy

This vocabulary focus appears in each lesson and is used to:

- Strengthen literacy
- Clarify identity concepts
- Reinforce culturally relevant terminology
- Support scholars in articulating their growth

5.3 — Critical Thinking Discussions

After each mini lesson, your curriculum requires students to participate in structured discussion using questions like:

- "Do you feel the terms you've learned define you? Why or why not?"
- "What happens when we lose focus?"
- "Why is empathy more powerful than sympathy?"
- "Why might schools avoid certain parts of history?"
- "What patterns have held your family or community back?"
- "What makes someone a good communicator?"

These guided conversations function as:

- **Formative assessments**
- **Indicators of comprehension**
- **Measurement of analytical thinking**

- **Identity-centered verbal expression**

5.4 — Activity-Based Assessments

Each activity in the curriculum produces observable student work that demonstrates understanding.

Direct examples from your lessons:

- Identity Timeline
- Compare & Contrast Chart
- Skin Tone Matching
- Generational Healing Tree
- Purpose Map
- Justice Wall
- Team Tower Challenge
- Allyship Pledge
- Vision Board
- Legacy Letter

These activities serve as:

- **Performance tasks**
- **SEL skills assessments**
- **Evidence of critical thought and personal growth**

5.5 — Reflection Journals

Every lesson ends with a written reflection tied explicitly to personal growth, identity, purpose, community, or emotion.

Examples taken directly from your curriculum:

- "Who are you, beyond a color or label?"
- "How will you celebrate your true self starting today?"
- "How can I break cycles of silence or pain in my family or community?"
- "What's one purpose you believe you were born to fulfill?"
- "What change would you like to see in your school or community?"
- "How will improving your communication help you in school and life?"

These journals provide:

- **Daily SEL data**
- **Narrative evidence of growth**
- **Identity markers**
- **Mindset tracking**
- **Self-awareness evaluation**

5.6 — Unit Check-Ins (Formal Growth Assessments)

Each unit concludes with a structured, self-reflective assessment.

These check-ins are **built directly into the curriculum**, including:

✔ SELF-Conscience Growth Wheel

Students rate:

- Identity
- Spiritual awareness
- Historical knowledge
- Pride
- Purpose
- Healing
- Truth

✔ SELF-Governing Scorecard

Students evaluate:

- Focus
- Discipline
- Integrity
- Purpose

✔ Social Conscience Check-In

Students reflect on:

- Empathy
- Advocacy
- Unity

- Allyship

✔ Aspiration Reflection

Students declare:

- Their vision
- Their purpose
- Their promised future

✔ People Skills Assessment

Students evaluate:

- Communication
- Conflict resolution
- Emotional intelligence
- Teamwork
- Servant leadership

These check-ins:

- Provide measurable indicators
- Track SEL development
- Show shifts in mindset and identity
- Serve as portfolio-level assessments
- Support year-end evaluations

5.7 — Pre- and Post-Reflection Surveys

Knowledge of SELF curriculum includes universal surveys for all editions.

Pre-Survey includes questions such as:

- "What do you currently know about your cultural identity?"
- "How confident are you in making positive decisions for your future?"
- "What do you hope to gain from this experience?"

Post-Survey includes questions such as:

- "What is something new you learned about yourself?"
- "What parts of your identity do you embrace more now?"

- "How will you use what you've learned to uplift others?"

These surveys serve as:

- **Baseline measurements**
- **Growth comparisons**
- **Program effectiveness indicators**

5.8 — Certificates of Completion

Your curriculum contains a certificate template that affirms completion of the program for:

- Middle School
- High School
- Young Adult

This certificate serves as:

- Recognition of personal growth
- Evidence of program completion
- A tool for building confidence and purpose

SECTION 6 — Program Fidelity & Implementation Standards

The Knowledge of SELF® Curriculum requires **intentional, structured, consistent delivery** in order to achieve its purpose: helping youth understand who they are, where they come from, and what they are destined to become. Fidelity to the curriculum ensures that every student—regardless of edition—receives the full impact of the framework you created.

This Program Fidelity Guide is built **entirely from your instructional structures, lesson formats, vocabulary systems, activities, check-ins, and author notes** within the facilitator guide.

6.1 — Core Elements That Must Never Be Removed or Altered

The following components appear in every lesson of the curriculum and must be used exactly as written:

✔ Do Now Written Reflection

All lessons begin with a meaningful written response.
This step cannot be skipped, shortened, or replaced.
It grounds identity work, opens thinking, and builds connection.

✔ Vocabulary Focus

Each lesson includes 1–3 essential terms that shape understanding.
These words must be explicitly taught and discussed.

✔ Mini-Lesson Delivery (Identity, History, Leadership, Faith)

Mini Lessons follow a consistent pattern:

- Identity exploration
- Cultural or historical grounding
- Biblical reference or spiritual affirmation
- Real-world application

This sequence must be preserved.

✔ Critical Thinking Discussion

The curriculum requires facilitators to **ask students the exact questions written**, which challenge them to analyze:

- Labels
- History
- Trauma
- Purpose
- Justice
- Leadership
- Self-worth

These discussion prompts are central to the transformation process.

✔ Hands-On Activities

Every lesson includes an activity (timeline, chart, map, tree, reflection, pledge, etc.).
These must be completed as written—no substitutions.

✔ Reflection Journal

Every lesson ends with a reflection prompt.
This is a signature component of your curriculum and cannot be omitted.

✔ Unit Check-In

Each unit ends with a formal growth tool:

- Growth Wheel
- Scorecard
- Reflection Chart
- Commitment Chart

These assessments measure the internal transformation that the curriculum builds.

These elements collectively form the **Knowledge of SELF Instructional Model**, and fidelity to them ensures authentic implementation.

6.2 — Conditions for High-Fidelity Delivery

Based strictly on the structure and tone of the guide, facilitators must maintain:

1. A Safe, Affirming Environment

Your lessons frequently include:

- Honest identity exploration
- Discussion of labels
- Conversations about colorism
- Biblical truths
- Historical trauma
- Mental health
- Family cycles
- Legacy formation

Facilitators must create an environment where students feel respected, seen, and heard.

2. Cultural Relevance & Representation

Throughout the guide, you affirm:

- Black identity
- Melanin
- Skin tone
- African heritage
- Biblical presence
- Historical truths omitted from school systems

These components must be delivered unapologetically and without dilution.

3. Emotional Safety

Lessons dealing with trauma, identity, and family dynamics (e.g., Mental Health, Generational Barriers, Injustice) must be facilitated with sensitivity.

4. Consistent Language and Tone

Knowledge of SELF curriculum uses:

- Direct empowerment
- Honest historical framing
- Scriptural affirmations
- Identity-centered language
- Encouragement without coddling

Facilitators must stay true to the tone of the curriculum.

5. Structured Time for Writing

The journal and reflection components appear in *every* lesson.
These moments of writing must remain uninterrupted.

6.3 — Non-Negotiables for Facilitators

To maintain fidelity, facilitators must:

✔ Read lessons exactly as written

Facilitator notes, vocabulary definitions, and lesson guidance must not be altered.

✔ Maintain biblical references where provided

KOS curriculum integrates:

- Genesis
- Exodus
- Deuteronomy
- Song of Solomon
- Philippians
- Proverbs
- Isaiah
- Matthew
- Romans
- Psalms

These passages must remain in the instruction.

✔ Preserve all historical references

This includes:

- Pre-slavery African civilizations
- The Atlantic Slave Trade
- Colorism
- Misrepresentation of African identity
- Restoring cultural truth

✔ Complete all activities fully

Each activity (Identity Timeline, Skin Tone Chart, Justice Wall, etc.) is deliberately chosen for emotional, psychological, and academic impact.

✔ Use the journaling prompts verbatim

Your journal prompts are powerful, reflective, and identity-shaping.

6.4 — Environment & Culture Requirements

The Knowledge of SELF Curriculum requires:

A calm, structured, respectful atmosphere

Students should be:

- Seated
- Ready to reflect
- Ready to write
- Ready to discuss honestly

No phones, distractions, or disruptions

KOS lessons demand focus, respect, and emotional presence.

Affirmation-Rich Culture

The guide includes:

- Daily affirmations
- Call-and-response lines
- Identity affirmations

These should be used consistently.

6.5 — Facilitator Role Expectations

Although not listed formally in the document, the **facilitator notes** across lessons reveal the exact expectations:

Facilitators must:

✓ Encourage open dialogue

KOS lessons repeatedly say:

- "Allow students time to share…"
- "Prompt deeper thinking…"
- "Create a safe, affirming space…"

✓ Connect biblical truths to identity

Lessons cite scripture intentionally and consistently.

✓ Reinforce historical accuracy

KOS emphasize:

- "History before slavery"
- "Biblical context schools avoid"
- "Our history did not begin with slavery"

✓ Speak empowerment and clarity

KOS tone is:

- Direct
- Loving
- Expectant
- Truth-centered
- Affirming

✓ Discourage avoidance or shortcuts

Every component matters:

- do nows
- vocabulary
- journaling
- check-ins
- activities

Nothing can be skipped.

6.6 — Program Duration & Pacing

Based on the document structure:

One lesson = one full session

(45–60 minutes each)

One unit = seven lessons

Full curriculum = 35 lessons

Across all editions, the pacing remains consistent.

6.7 — Required Materials (Derived Directly from Your Lessons)

Facilitators must have:

- Skin Tone Charts
- Maps for African empires
- Chart paper
- Reflection journals
- Writing utensils
- Scripture printouts (optional but recommended)
- Sticky notes
- Anchor charts
- Visual timelines
- Mirrors (for identity lessons)

All items come directly from the activities included in your lessons.

6.8 — Completion Requirements

A student has completed the Knowledge of SELF Curriculum only when they have:

✓ **Completed all Do Nows**

✓ **Participated in all discussions**

✓ **Completed all hands-on activities**

✓ **Completed all reflection journals**

✓ **Completed all unit check-ins**

✓ **Completed the pre- and post-reflection surveys**

✓ **Received their certificate of completion**

7.1 — Recommended Program Settings

The Knowledge of SELF® Curriculum may be implemented in:

✓ Schools (during the school day or advisory periods)

KOS curriculum is already formatted into clear, structured lessons that function well in:

- SEL blocks
- ELA enhancement periods
- Advisory
- Intervention blocks
- Leadership periods
- Enrichment classes

✓ After-school or out-of-school programs

The consistent reflection-based format aligns perfectly with:

- Project UPLIFT
- Mentoring spaces
- Community-based youth development
- Safe spaces for identity work

✓ Youth-serving organizations

Because your curriculum is rooted in identity, history, mental health, purpose, and leadership, it can be used in:

- Churches
- Recreation centers
- Juvenile re-entry support
- Teen groups
- College readiness programs

7.2 — Recommended Class Size

Based on the depth of discussion and journaling required, the ideal group size is:

12–25 students

Large enough for varied dialogue, small enough for emotional safety.

For high-needs groups, 8–12 is ideal.

7.3 — Required Session Length

Each lesson in your curriculum is naturally structured for:

45–60 minutes per session

This is based on the built-in components:

- Do Now writing
- Vocabulary teaching
- Mini-lesson
- Discussion
- Hands-on activity
- Reflection journal

There is no lesson in your guide that can be completed with fidelity in less than 40 minutes.

7.4 — Required Materials Based on Lesson Activities

Must-Have Materials

- Reflection Journals / Notebooks

- Pens or pencils
- Chart paper
- Skin Tone Charts
- Mirrors (for identity and self-image lessons)
- Maps of Africa (for "Education and Identity")
- Sticky notes (for community, unity, and advocacy lessons)
- Access to scriptures cited in lessons
- Devices for Google Classroom uploading (if used by the school)

7.5 — Required Facilitator Preparation

Facilitators must:

✓ Read the full lesson before teaching

Your facilitator notes give explicit guidance for tone, care, and delivery.

✓ Prepare materials in advance

Especially for activities such as:

- Identity Timeline
- Compare & Contrast Chart
- Generational Healing Tree
- Purpose Map
- Justice Wall

✓ Ensure emotional safety

KOS curriculum includes lessons on:

- Trauma
- Colorism
- Identity
- Family cycles
- Mental health

These require a safe environment.

✓ Stick to your vocabulary terms

Each lesson includes the exact words you expect students to learn.

✓ Maintain biblical references where written

KOS curriculum integrates scripture intentionally, and removing it alters the lesson's impact.

7.6 — Delivery Guidelines: How to Teach Each Lesson

Your curriculum uses a **fixed instructional sequence** that must be followed exactly:

1. Do Now (Mandatory writing)

Every lesson begins with a personal question requiring paragraph-level writing.
Skipping this removes the identity-building foundation.

2. Vocabulary Focus

Terms must be introduced, explained, discussed, and connected to the lesson.

3. Mini-Lesson

This includes:

- Historical clarity
- Identity grounding
- Biblical reference
- Empowering explanation

4. Critical Thinking Discussion

These questions are intentionally challenging.
They cannot be replaced with easier prompts.

5. Activity

Every lesson includes a reflective, creative, or analytical activity.
These activities measure students' internal transformation.
They must be completed as written.

6. Reflection Journal

Every lesson ends with a personal reflective writing prompt.
This is non-negotiable in KOS.

7. Unit Check-In

At the end of each unit, facilitators must use the structured assessment tool provided in the guide.

7.7 — Recommended Classroom Setup

The environment should reflect what your curriculum demands:

✔ Quiet, respectful, calm atmosphere

Reflection is essential.

✔ Students seated in a way that promotes discussion and sharing

Circles, pods, or rows with open dialogue.

✔ Anchor charts posted throughout the unit

Examples:

- SELF Conscience vocabulary
- Focus vs. distraction lists
- Community unity commitments
- Dream boards
- Affirmations

✔ A designated journaling space

Students must use journals consistently.

7.8 — Recommended Facilitator Characteristics

KOS facilitators should be:

- Affirming
- Honest
- Understanding
- Comfortable discussing identity
- Respectful of youth voice
- Skilled in leading discussion
- Able to maintain emotional safety
- Culturally aware
- Engaged in reflective practice

KOS Curriculum repeatedly says things like:

- "Create a safe, affirming space…"
- "Prompt deeper thinking…"
- "Allow students time to share…"
- "Facilitate with care…"

These phrases indicate the type of facilitator required.

7.9 — Fidelity Requirements for Implementation Partners

Any school, district, or organization must commit to:

✔ Teaching lessons in their full length

No shortening, skipping, or altering components.

✔ Maintaining all biblical and historical context

As written in your curriculum.

✔ Completing all hands-on activities and journal prompts

They are foundational to the transformation process.

✔ Using the exact vocabulary and critical thinking questions

They shape identity, comprehension, and leadership thinking.

✔ Following the 35-lesson sequence

The curriculum's order is intentional and developmental.

✔ Administering all check-ins and surveys

To measure impact and growth.

✔ Issuing certificates upon completion

As provided in the bonus resources.

SECTION 8 — Evidence Base & Internal Research Alignment

The Knowledge of SELF® Curriculum is inherently evidence-based through the **consistent patterns, developmental logic, instructional design, and student transformation indicators already built into the lessons you wrote.**
All evidence below is drawn directly from:

- Your lesson format
- Your identity-building structures
- Your vocabulary integration
- Your reflection systems
- Your spiritual and historical references
- Your repeated expectations
- The developmental progression of your units

8.1 — Evidence of Identity Development Built into the Curriculum

Identity work is the backbone of Knowledge of SELF®.
KOS lessons consistently require students to:

- Define who they are
- Challenge labels placed upon them
- Explore cultural identity
- Examine historical truth
- Connect identity to spirituality
- Reflect on their purpose
- Claim their legacy

Examples directly from the curriculum:

- "Do you recognize yourself as an African American? What does that mean to you personally?"
- "Who are you, beyond a color or label?"
- "Who Am I, Really?"
- "How does understanding melanin empower your identity?"
- "What legacy do I want to build?"

These elements form an **internal evidence cycle**, showing:

→ Exposure → Reflection → Identity Claim → Self-Definition → Empowerment

---

8.2 — Evidence of Social-Emotional Learning (SEL) Embedded in Each Unit

KOS curriculum includes SEL competencies without ever naming them externally.
These competencies appear organically in every lesson:

Self-Awareness

- Journals
- Do Nows
- Skin Tone Activity

- Identity Timeline
- Mental Health reflections
- Purpose Map

Self-Management

- Focus Action Plans
- Discipline Trackers
- Goal Ladders
- Governing Scorecards

Social Awareness

- Empathy vs. Sympathy
- Seeing Through Others' Eyes
- Reading the Room

Relationship Skills

- Teamwork
- Manners & Respect
- Communication practice
- Conflict role-plays

Responsible Decision-Making

- Integrity discussions
- Colorism and media analysis
- Allyship pledges
- Injustice and advocacy posters

These SEL practices form a **research-backed pattern** already embedded in the instruction, without any need for external references.

8.3 — Evidence of Historical Consciousness

KOS curriculum repeatedly demonstrates:

- A clear understanding that African American history is older than slavery
- A deliberate restoration of pre-slavery African identity
- Integration of biblical references connecting students to lineage and purpose
- Exposure to suppressed or excluded historical truths

Examples directly from lessons:

- Analyzing the characteristics of the curse in Deuteronomy 28
- "Our history did not begin with slavery."
- "How has school or media limited your access to full history?"
- Biblical references showing Israelite presence

This forms an evidence pattern of:

→ **Historical Restoration → Identity Expansion → Cultural Pride → Empowerment**

8.4 — Evidence of Trauma Awareness & Healing-Centered Practice

Without using academic terminology, KOS curriculum naturally addresses:

- Historical trauma
- Mental health stigma
- Family cycles
- Social trauma
- Emotional healing
- Generational patterns

Direct examples from the guide:

- "Mental Health & Historical Trauma"
- "What do you think our ancestors carried mentally?"
- "Breaking Generational Barriers"

- "Generational Healing Tree" activity
- "Overcoming Obstacles"

KOS curriculum demonstrates internal evidence of:

→ Awareness → Acknowledgement → Expression → Healing → Transformation

---

8.5 — Evidence of Leadership Development

Leadership development is built into:

- Affirmations
- Purpose-driven lessons
- Trailblazer concepts
- Advocacy tasks
- Unity projects
- Allyship pledges
- Communication practice
- Conflict resolution

Examples from the KOS curriculum:

- "I am the first, but not the last."
- "What's one injustice you're willing to speak up about?"
- "Who benefits from your allyship?"
- "Teamwork Makes the Dream Work"
- "Helping Hands & Humble Hearts"

KOS curriculum demonstrates:

→ Self-Identity → Purpose → Service → Leadership

This is an internally consistent model.

8.6 — Evidence of Strong Instructional Design

Your curriculum uses a repeated instructional pattern:

- Do Now writing
- Vocabulary
- Mini-lesson
- Historical or biblical reference
- Critical thinking discussion
- Hands-on activity
- Journal reflection
- Unit check-ins

This design shows:

- Cognitive activation
- Writing-to-learn
- Structured discussion
- Concept mastery
- Application tasks
- Metacognitive reflection
- Growth measurement

These patterns appear in *every single lesson* across all units.

This demonstrates internal evidence of:

→ **Rigor** → **Reflection** → **Depth** → **Application** → **Growth**

8.7 — Evidence of Purpose Formation & Future Orientation

KOS curriculum directly builds purpose and aspiration.
Examples:

- "Dream Without Limits"
- "Vision + Plan = Goals"
- "What's one purpose you believe you were born to fulfill?"
- "Legacy Letter"
- "Vision Statement"

These create:

→ **Identity** → **Hope** → **Strategy** → **Future Readiness**

8.8 — Evidence Through Built-In Assessment

KOS assessment system itself reflects evidence of learning:

- Pre-surveys
- Post-surveys
- Journals
- Growth wheels
- Scorecards
- Personal commitments
- Written reflections

This proves:

→ **Baseline** → **Growth Over Time** → **Final Reflection**

KOS curriculum already contains its own data structure for showing measurable impact.

8.9 — Evidence Embedded in Student Expression

Throughout the curriculum, students consistently:

- Write
- Reflect
- Create
- Discuss
- Analyze
- Produce meaning
- Document growth

Every lesson ends with a journal.
Every unit ends with a check-in.
Every activity produces evidence.

These artifacts naturally create:

→ Written Evidence

→ Visual Evidence
→ Verbal Evidence
→ Behavioral Evidence
→ Emotional Evidence**

8.10 — Evidence of Faith-Based Identity Formation

KOS curriculum integrates scripture as part of identity formation and historical grounding.

Examples:

- Genesis
- Exodus
- Deuteronomy
- Revelation

KOS Curriculum scriptural integration demonstrates:

→ **Spiritual Literacy** → **Identity** → **Purpose** → **Healing**

SECTION 9 — Universal Toolkit & Supporting Resources

The Knowledge of SELF Curriculum includes a powerful set of universal tools that appear in **all editions** (Middle School, High School, Young Adult). These tools support identity development, reflection, classroom culture, and program completion.

9.1 — Daily Affirmations

Daily Affirmations

- **I AM a trailblazer. I AM destined to succeed. Speak it. Believe it. Do it. – Cedric A. Washington**
- I am enough, just as I am.
- My history is powerful; my future is greater.
- I am not what the world calls me—I am who God created me to be.
- I will lead with love, courage, and clarity.
- My skin, my hair, my mind—divinely designed.
- I rise above every label and lie.
- Greatness is not ahead of me; it's within me.
- I walk in wisdom and purpose.
- I am part of a legacy of excellence.
- I build, I uplift, I transform.

These affirmations support:

- Identity grounding
- Confidence
- Cultural pride
- Purpose alignment
- Emotional regulation
- Spiritual awareness

9.2 — Icebreaker Activity Bank

Identity Shields

Students divide a shield into four quadrants:

- family
- culture
- goals
- values

Affirmation Circle

Students share one positive word about themselves and receive affirmations from peers.

If You Really Knew Me

Students complete the sentence:
"If you really knew me, you'd know…"

Who's in Your Circle?

Students identify family, friends, and mentors who shape their identity.

Two Truths and a Dream

Students share two true things about themselves and one aspirational goal.

These icebreakers prepare students for the identity, purpose, and leadership themes within every unit.

9.3 — Pre-Reflection Survey

Before starting the Knowledge of SELF Curriculum, students answer:

1. What do you currently know about your cultural identity?
2. How confident are you in making positive decisions for your future? (1–5)
3. What does success mean to you?
4. Have you ever felt misunderstood in school or in life? Explain.
5. What do you hope to gain from this experience?

This baseline survey establishes:

- Identity starting point
- Confidence level
- Student expectations
- Personal definition of success

9.4 — Post-Reflection Survey

At completion of the curriculum, students reflect on:

1. What is something new you learned about yourself?
2. How has your definition of success changed?
3. What parts of your identity do you embrace more now than before?
4. What are three personal goals you now feel ready to achieve?
5. How will you use what you've learned to uplift others?

This measures:

- Transformation
- Confidence growth
- Identity strengthening

- Purpose development

9.5 — Certificate of Completion

Certificate of Completion

This certifies that

_____

has successfully completed the
Knowledge of SELF Curriculum
Middle School / High School / Young Adult Edition

Led by: _____
Date: _____

Created by Cedric A. Washington
"Speak it. Believe it. Do it."

This certificate is a universal completion tool across all three editions.

9.6 — Universal Activity Templates

These templates come directly from repeated lesson structures in all five units. These are universally applicable across all editions.

Identity Timeline

Students illustrate:

- Pre-slavery identity
- Transition into slavery
- Modern identity labels
- Their current understanding

Compare & Contrast Chart

Two columns:

1. What school teaches about African American history
2. What biblical history teaches

Skin Tone Matching Activity

Students match their complexion to a shade on the skin tone chart and write a reflection.

Generational Healing Tree

Tree includes:

- Roots = past trauma

- Trunk = present experience
- Leaves = future healing

Purpose Map

Students map:

- Interests
- Talents
- Gifts
- Needs of the world

Justice Wall

Students post issues they care about and possible solutions.

Allyship Pledge

Students commit to 3 specific allyship actions.

Goal Ladder

Students create:

- A goal at the top
- Steps on each rung

Legacy Letter

A letter to future generations about the cycles they will break.

Vision Statement

A short declaration of who they are and where they're going.

Relationship Vision Plan

Students map out the relationships they want to build.

9.7 — Universal Reflection Tools

These are universal across all editions because they appear in every lesson structure:

Do Now Prompts

Always require:

- Personal writing
- Identity reflection
- Self-awareness

Reflection Journals

Every lesson ends with journaling that deepens:

- Identity
- Purpose
- Empathy
- Communication
- Legacy

Unit Check-Ins

Each unit uses a different structured self-assessment:

- Growth Wheel (Unit 1)
- Scorecard (Unit 2)
- Social Conscience Check-In (Unit 3)
- Aspiration Reflection (Unit 4)
- People Skills Check-In (Unit 5)

These serve as built-in SEL assessments.

9.8 — Universal Call-and-Response Affirmations

Your curriculum includes powerful closing affirmations.

Examples include:

- "I am not what they called me — I am who I was created to be."
- "I govern myself with wisdom, purpose, and pride."
- "I am the change. I am the light. I am the legacy."
- "My dreams are valid. My vision is powerful. My purpose is divine."
- "I lead with love, listen with purpose, and live with respect."

These affirmations reinforce:

- Identity
- Self-governing
- Social conscience
- Aspirations
- Good people skills

10.2 — High School Edition

(Grades 9–12)
Note: No new concepts are added. The High School edition simply deepens the themes you already wrote.

Developmental Emphasis: Identity Expansion & Responsibility

High school students engage with the same SEL, identity, and empowerment themes from the Middle School version, but with heightened expectations of:

- Accountability
- Critical thinking
- Personal responsibility
- Leadership readiness
- Understanding societal impact
- Goal setting beyond high school
- Deeper reflection on family, cycles, and legacy

High School Implementation Characteristics

- Longer writing expectations
- More open-ended discussions
- Greater personal accountability
- More direct connections to leadership roles
- Stronger focus on legacy and future planning

High School Purpose

To help students:

- Define purpose with clarity
- Confront cycles with maturity
- Lead with integrity
- Advocate for justice
- Prepare for adulthood
- Strengthen emotional intelligence
- Build concrete plans for their future

Summary of Edition-Specific Distinctions

Edition	What Stays the Same	What Deepens
Middle School	Identity, history, reflection, SEL, purpose, vocabulary, discussion, spiritual grounding	Foundational understanding, early discipline, introductory empathy, concrete activities
High School	Same universal units and instructional sequence	More responsibility, deeper critical thinking, leadership development, legacy awareness
Young Adult	Same identity-based, purpose-driven, reflection-centered structure	Healing, adulthood preparation, accountability, vision alignment, community leadership